ANCHOR BOOKS

MUM'S THE WORD

Edited by

Steph Park-Pirie

First published in Great Britain in 2004 by
ANCHOR BOOKS
Remus House,
Coltsfoot Drive,
Peterborough, PE2 9JX
Telephone (01733) 898102

All Rights Reserved

Copyright Contributors 2004

SB ISBN 1 84418 361 0

FOREWORD

Anchor Books is a small press, established in 1992, with the aim of promoting readable poetry to as wide an audience as possible.

We hope to establish an outlet for writers of poetry who may have struggled to see their work in print.

The poems presented here have been selected from many entries, and as always editing proved to be a difficult task.

I trust this selection will delight and please the authors and all those who enjoy reading poetry.

Steph Park-Pirie
Editor

CONTENTS

The Childminder	Christopher John Symonds	1
An Ode To My Mother	Eileen M Hailes	2
A Mother Remembers	Julie Brown	3
Heather	Rebecca Mifsud	4
Winged Memories	Janet Bamber	5
Mother	Diana Daley	6
Poem For Mum	Richard Morris	7
My Mother	Lyndsay Lynch	8
The Human Dynamo	Bob Vincent	9
My Mum	Jenna Gormal	10
Mum	Martin & April Stuart-MacRae	11
I Will Send Your Flowers To Heaven	Clare Saffell	12
Dear Mum . . .	Christian Barnett	14
My Mum's Ways	Kelly Barnett	15
Mum	Stephen Oliver	16
What Mothers Are . . .	Tanya Ozkan	17
No Better Way	S Sessions	18
A Mother's Love	Liz Abbott	19
Grace	Peter Castle	20
Mum	Jennifer Wright	21
Mum	Ruth Walker	22
My Mum Is . . .	Maxine T Hartley	24
Mum	Sid Harris	25
My Mother	Norman S Brittain	26
For You Mum	Linda Brown	27
Memory Lane	Norah Nelson	28
Emma's Mum	Pearl Devereux	29
For My Mom, With Love	Jacqui Beddow	30
For My Mother	Bob Crossley	31
Mum - Server	G Knapton	32
Lai Yung	Mei Yuk Wong	34
For My Mother	Anne James	35
Poems For Mum	Coleen Bradshaw	36
Hard Lines	Nayyer Ali	37
My Treasure	Christina Marie Dunworth	38

To My Life's Giver	V Malavolta	39
Mother	Mack Senge	40
Mother's Poem	Gary Morton	41
Barbara	Laura Maxwell	42
A Mother's Day Ode To A Special Mum	Sharyn Waters	43
Mum	Gillian Robson	44
Mum	Ruth Mclean	45
Thank You Mum	Sophie Mir	46
My Mum	Ester Golding-Webb	47
Mother's Touch	Ellen Simmons	48
Poem For My Mum	Janice Cameron	50
Mum	Pamela Holt	51
An Angel With God's Gift	Nicola Fulstow	52
Mother	Shirley May Croxford	53
My Mum	Elizabeth Marshall	54
Mothering Sunday	A F Hiscocks	55
The Very Greatest	Toby Harwin	56
A Mother's Love Is Worth Cherishing	Catherine Keal	58
A Poem For Mum	Matthew Willbye	59
Mum	Tony Turner	60
Mother	Windsor Hopkins	61
A Mother's Touch	Lil Bordessa	62
Being A Mother	Mary Davies	63
One In A Million - My Mum	Lorraine A Robinson	64
Mum	Susan Jenner	65
Mother	Gary Bil	66
My Mam	Cindy Webster	67
I Love My Mum	Trudy Marie Burge	68
✗ Mother	Hugh H Foulkes	69
Mothering Sunday	Alan J Morgan	70
Mum	Jack Thurgar	71
Visiting My Mum	Kevin Godfrey	72
Mother's Day	Carol Kaye	73
She Is Nice To Me	Ogbodo John Obinna	74
A Belated Message	Ann G Wallace	75
Mum	John Paulley	76

Love	M Wilcox	77
Requiem For Mum	Jean Wallington	78
My Mum	K Christie	79
A Love That Must Be Trusted	Marjorie Picton	80
Mother's Blessing	Rebecca Guest	81
A Miner's Wife, My Mother	John Pegg	82
The Queen Of Creation Be She	Mark Anthony Noble	83
Mothers	R Weedall	84
Mother	B W Ballard	86
Grand Gestures	Tiffany Little	88
My Mother	Robert Basham	89
My Mother	P K Janaky	90
A Glimpse Of Heaven	Pearl M Burdock	91
A Family Treasure	Julia Pegg	92
Mum	Charlene Tate	93
IOU Mum	R Bennett	94
My Fantastic Mum	Nigel Astell	96

THE CHILDMINDER

I think you have done really well,
Probably more than words can tell,
How you stayed at home for your baby to see,
He'll appreciate that at 53.
It was hard for you to give up your job,
You had a future there and the things that count,
Now you're home making cups of tea,
He'll appreciate that at 53.
'Listen with Mother' was a really good programme,
Some will remember it, some will not,
Did we listen to Alma Cogan,
As you cared for me in the cot?
But I thank you Mum for taking the time,
At least you gave me the chance to feel fine,
I appreciate that and for all that you do,
Maybe one day I will do the same for you.

Christopher John Symonds

AN ODE TO MY MOTHER

Right from the cradle you stood by my side, through thick and thin,
Could I have gained that quiet strength that came from you within?
From tiny babe you held my hand, to little girl I grew,
You guided me through most of life and taught me all you knew,
I loved you so, but didn't show how very much I cared,
But you were there to soothe my fears, with love you always shared,
You sacrificed for Dad and I, yourself you thought of last,
Our words or deeds could not repay, your giving was so vast,
Your patience and your kindness when life went sad astray,
Your gentleness and quiet support drove all the hurt away,
My world was shattered when you died, I never could foresee,
My life without you, Mother dear, you were the world to me,
Although I cannot hold you close, nor kiss your gentle brow,
I feel deep down inside me that you know my thoughts somehow,
For as I sit here quietly, my dreams with me abide,
I sense an inner peace and know you're still here by my side.

Eileen M Hailes

A MOTHER REMEMBERS

From the moment I held you
so perfect and sweet,
my cup of happiness
was at last complete.

I watched you grow
into a lovely child,
though not always
so meek and mild.

A typical young boy
you grew big and strong.
In my heart I knew
it couldn't be long.

As the years passed
we had to part,
another young lady
had stolen your heart.

Enjoy your love,
to each other be true,
and always remember
I love both of you.

Julie Brown

HEATHER

For giving me hope,
When I had none,
For giving me strength,
When I was falling,
For hearing my words
That needed saying,
For pushing me onwards,
When I felt like staying . . .
I thank you.

For words given in love,
For the words left unsaid,
For the days in the sunshine,
For the days in the rain,
For sharing my happiness,
For feeling my pain . . .
I thank you.

For the tears that you cried,
For the times that you worried,
For the sacrifices you made quietly,
For cheering me on when I've had to fight,
For walking with me in the darkness
And dancing with me in the light . . .
I thank you.

For loving me unconditionally,
    I thank you.
For your patience,
    I thank you.

For your kindness,
    I thank you.
For the gift of your motherhood . . . I thank you.

Rebecca Mifsud

WINGED MEMORIES

Mum, I saw a butterfly today.
It's November the tenth,
And a Red Admiral
Came fluttering over the garden.
I couldn't believe it.
Butterflies in November!

At first I thought it was an autumn leaf
Whirling around,
Its bright colours catching the light.
Then I realised
It was a late, solitary straggler;
A flashback to summer.

Do you remember when you stayed with us
The summer of nineteen ninety-one?
We had eight weeks of old-style weather;
Long, dry, hot sunny days.
You dozed and dreamed in the shade
At the bottom of the garden.

When you awoke, we drank tea,
And watched the butterflies
Drinking rapturously of the buddleias.
We heard the soothing hum of bees,
Hoverflies, and a myriad tiny insects
Moving among the flowering herbs.

Mum, I saw a butterfly today,
And thought of those golden days
We spent together.
Next year I will watch the butterflies
With your great grandchildren,
And we will think of you.

Janet Bamber

MOTHER

She is gentle, sweet and kind
Another like her would be hard to find
To her children she is strong
Teaching them right from wrong
Showing each one things to do
Imparting to them her point of view
Giving a love that's really meant
Hoping they grow up strong and decent
And live their lives right to the end
Loving each other as relation and friend
Words of wisdom on how to live
Words that only a mother can give
Give to her children when they part
Give to her children from her heart.

Diana Daley

POEM FOR MUM

From early days, baby to teens
Your life as an adult to come
One person who's there, through pain and joy
It's the one, we all call 'Mum'.

Throughout life, right or wrong
She will take our side, no questions asked
Her love for us, no rules apply
Any doubters, she will take to task.

Always stand our corner, she will cry our tears
All the pains of life, she will share
When our hearts are broken, our life feels sad
Then Mum is always there.

We all, only have one real mum
A true friend, who's there for life
And we use her strengths and finer points
When we men are choosing a wife.

So for all my thoughts and loving words
All for a mother I truly adore
God bless the creation of this fine breed
For my love, is for evermore.

Richard Morris

MY MOTHER

In a blink of an eye the years have gone by,
And what I've put you through I think with a sigh.
The teenage years were the worst for me
And what I needed, only my mother could see.
You guided me through all those hard times and more
With strength and dignity the hardships you bore.
I know you are only ever a phone call away
And I love you more with each passing day.
You are the one who's been with me since birth
And showed me the beauty of this heavenly Earth.
Simple and pure like the white of a dove
Best describes this daughter's love.

Lyndsay Lynch

THE HUMAN DYNAMO
(A song for my mum, Maggie)

Born and raised in Plymouth
a Plymouthian through and through
you can tell that in her accent
especially when she's had a few

Some people call her Maggie
I just call her Mum
she's like a human dynamo
never stopping till it's done.

She came to Jersey seeking fortune
but met poor old Dad instead
thirty years later
she still makes sure he's fed

Some people call her Maggie
I just call her Mum
she's like a human dynamo
never stopping till it's done.

Four babies came along
And beauties at that
survived on picking potatoes
and had enough to feed the cat

She's ironing with her left hand
she's cooking with her right
finishes everything just in time
it's 'EastEnders' tonight

So God bless you Maggie
we're proud of the job you've done
raise a glass for the birthday girl
you're so lucky I'm your son!

Bob Vincent

MY MUM

Since I was born my mum has been there,
Picking me up when I'm down,
Never having the need to wear a frown.
Mum is loving and caring,
She is mine and she's precious,
Like antique glassware that belonged to Queen Elizabeth.

If I'm worried, Mum will make it better,
Mum will hug me and tell me that she will take care
Of whatever is the matter,
I know then that I will be safe because I can trust her.

Mum will even stay up with me till very late at night,
As she strokes my cheek I know that I'm alright,
These little things make me feel as happy as a kite
Making its way to the sky as it takes its first flight.

My mum is 'Superwoman'
She puts Superman to shame,
Mum does the things that really matter
Even if they're not lifesaving,
My mum cooks, my mum cleans,
My mum washes and irons,
My mum takes me to school,
Without any complaint, I think that's very cool!

My mum is a ray of sunshine that lights up my life,
My mum is like air to the lungs
She feels just right,
My mum is not fiction,
My mum is fact,
My mum is the best in the world,
Now I would like to see your mums beat that!

Jenna Gormal (13)

Mum

Mum, you're a pest
Kidding on, you're the best
You're fantastic, you're amazing, you're number one

If you were in a book, you'd get a tick
If you were flowers you'd be picked
You are loving, you are caring and you're fun

But sometimes you are bad
And you really make us sad
But we always say sorry and make up

Sometimes you nag on the phone
Or give a little moan
But you always know when to shut up

You're our guiding light
You help us when we fight
To us you're like a beautiful big white dove

We love you with all our heart
Hopefully we will never part
We've written this poem to show you all our love

We love you Mum.

Martin (5) & April Stuart-MacRae (10)

I Will Send Your Flowers To Heaven

My mother is the woman
Who feeds my soul with joy.
Her life is mine within me
Twinned tightly as we grow
From childhood through to womanhood
Close-knit and sealed combined.

Our thoughts are one
Our bones, the same
Our knowledge
Carried high
Beyond the frame
Of the photograph
That hangs
Upon the wall.

My mother is the woman
Who restores my peace of mind.
Her voice before the pips of time
Rock and cradle untold pain
In a booth that's made for one,
She settles me to sleep.

I will send your flowers to Heaven
Yellow petals cold with ice
Frosted into parchment
By your death in the golden sun
And I'll wait for the warmth
Of your breath of love
To restore
All brittle hope.

My mother is the woman
Who left me all alone
She cast me from her womb
To leave me drowning in her life,
Our twin souls lost, despairing
Ever searching for an ending.

Clare Saffell

DEAR MUM...

Dear Mum, I am here to say,
Thanks for keeping a roof over my head all day.
You never make me look uncool,
Go on, admit it, you so totally rule.
So far you have made me a perfect life,
No wonder Dad wanted you as a wife.
In my life you have played an important role,
You have made my life whole.

You're so nice, you should be a saint,
I love you so much, I think I'm going to faint.
Mum, you probably see,
If it wasn't for you I wouldn't be part of this family tree.
I hope you see me as a brilliant son,
I see you as a mum, full of fun.
You buy me books, games and toys,
You buy me clothes right for boys.

Your hobby is tidying the house,
From the upstairs toilet to the sewer mouse.
You tidy my bedroom,
If I gave you a brush and shovel, you'd just zoom.
Dear Mum, that's all I have to say,
Every day for me is a 'Mother's Day'.

Christian Barnett (11)

MY MUM'S WAYS

My mummy is so very great,
She's ready though she's always late,
It's me who holds her up I fear,
Hope she sheds not a single tear,
Mum comforts me when I am down,
She deserves to wear a crown,
She wears such old peculiar clothes,
She looks quite weird and yet she knows,
She has highlighted ruffled hair,
She knows and yet she doesn't care,
I feel her driving needs to improve,
For when she parks you have to move,
But if you knew how long it takes,
You'd think she drove with switched-on brakes,
I like it at meals when she wears a dress,
That's quite rare cos she makes a mess,
She puts her face cream on every night,
Oh my goodness, what a sight!
Always looking for wrinkles upon her face,
She doesn't know about her grace,
When she gets into a mood,
She gets quite bossy and quite rude,
But I love her all the same,
For if there is mischief I'm to blame,
I don't know what goes on in her mind,
But in the real world she is very kind.

Kelly Barnett (8)

Mum

A unique mother
with natural concern,
we're fortunate
that you care.

And as we walk
towards your home,
we love to know
you're there.

Your kindness is
day in, day out
just always
close to hand.

And as we sleep
your gentle praise
has helped us
understand.

Stephen Oliver

WHAT MOTHERS ARE . . .
(For my mum)

Mothers are super, mothers are great,
They're someone we should *never* hate.

Our mothers care and our mothers share.
They always try to make things fair.

After all their work throughout the year,
Their special day is finally here!

So, on this year's Mother's Day,
This is what I'd like to say:

'Mummy, Mummy, I love you.
When I'm here and when I'm there.
Mum, I love you everywhere.'

Tanya Ozkan

No Better Way

I have sat for many hours
Thinking long and hard
Sat in the kitchen
In the bathroom and the yard

All of this thinking
That is being done
Is on how I can show I care
After all I am your son

Despite all my efforts
Thinking myself black and blue
I still can't find a better way
Than saying, 'I love you!'

S Sessions

A Mother's Love

A mother's love is always there, in good times and in bad.
A love that gives me strength, for each and every dream I've had.
To lead the way, to show the light, if ever I feel low.
To share happiness and pleasure, for every joy that I will know.

A mother's love is always there, no matter where we are.
A love so strong and deep, keeps us together, near or far.
To know that you are there for me, to give, to love, to share.
I feel your arms around me, even when they are not there.

Now I have children of my own, to keep close to my heart.
I treasure even more the love you gave right from the start.
A love so unconditional, a love so real and true.
So Mum, I want to thank you, and say how much I love you too.

Liz Abbott

GRACE

I'd like to say a word about a friend of mine called Grace.
You'd know her if you met her by the smile upon her face.
If you tell her of your worries, she's sure to understand
And for anyone who needs it, she will lend a helping hand.

She's knocked about a bit, has Grace, as some of you may know.
She met with life's disasters and she gave them blow for blow.
When Hitler took it in his head to bomb old London's pride
Grace became a Red Cross nurse and took it in her stride.

She dodged about amid the blitz and if you ask her why,
'Well, someone had to do it,' is all that she'd reply.
And when the war was over, true to her golden rule,
Grace carried on as Matron in a children's nursery school.

When a matron who was 'qualified' arrived to run the place
The governors all said, 'Thank you very much and ta-ta Grace.'
It didn't get our Gracie down. She said, 'Well, it's a shame.
I'll have to help somebody else.' And a 'home help' she became.

But now she's getting on a bit and doesn't toil no more.
She's in an old folks hostel, number forty on the door.
And does she put her feet up, and does she take her ease?
She's singing with a bloomin' concert party, if you please!

She's helping to run jumble sales, still giving of her best.
She gads about in bingo halls and dances, full of zest.
And sometimes in the evening, when she finds her tasks are done,
She'll write a poem for printing in a mag called '141'!

Well, Grace is not the only one to pen a bit of verse.
There's some who do it better, and a lot who do it worse.
And this may not be very good but I hope it finds a place
To tell a bit about her, my mother, my friend Grace!

Peter Castle

Mum

You are me.
Looking at you,
I can see there are
Only years between us,
Only years to make us
Different people.
You are more than me,
My carer,
My friend,
My lifeline:
Alone without you,
I dare not imagine
Such an existence.
You are my maker.
My proud heart beats lovingly
With your blood.

Jennifer Wright (16)

Mum

She sits there day by day - silently - sometimes not so silently - yielding to the hands that care for her.
Passive, yet watching and listening.
What does she see? What does she hear?
What metamorphoses of image and sound occur before she gives thought to them?

I feed her. 'Open wide - good girl.'
This isn't right!
She is the child; I am the mother?
No!
I am the child; *she* is the mother.

How much longer, Lord . . . ?

I think I understand.
The celestial Hoover is out - everything must be spick and span for her arrival.

You should know, by the way, she won't just sit back and enjoy it - not Mum.
She'll be playing with the babies; cuddling the children - she was always so snugly.
She'll be making the salmon sandwiches - oh - and a nice cream sponge too.
She'll see the potential in a royal robe hanging on a steel hanger - 'This one will look nice on you dear - just try it.'
And she'll be right!

And she'll sing - you'll enjoy that, Lord.
You may have forgotten what her voice sounds like - it's been so long since she *really* sang.

I have to say it Lord - it doesn't matter if the place isn't spick and span.
Please don't wait too much longer.
I want to think of my mum as Mum again;
in her proper body - singing out to you - 'I'd rather have Jesus.'
Not the fragile shell that now encases her.
Not the mumbled, unintelligible words escaping, thin, dry lips.

But Jennie - Mum.

Ruth Walker

MY MUM IS . . .

My mum is the sunshine on a rainy day.
My mum is the one who advises the way.
My mum is the one who loves me when I do wrong.
My mum is the skylark singing the song.

My mum is warm when it's snowy and cold
My mum is the one to say when I need to be told.
My mum is the magic when I hurt inside.
My mum is the rules by which I abide.

My mum is cuddly and holds tight.
The voice to praise me when I'm right.
My mum is the rainbow in trouble and strife.
My mum is the one who gave me life.

Maxine T Hartley

Mum

How do you describe an angel
Who was put here on this Earth
Who comforted, caressed and protected me
From the moment of my birth?

Her loving eyes, her precious smile
Though many years we have been apart
Stay with me every single day
And are embedded in my heart

No one ever saw her pain
Or the crosses she had to bear
They were hidden behind a mystic smile
And a nature beyond compare

Growing older I now understand
The magnificence of her love
Endorsed by friends and family
And I am sure by God above

If I could roll back the sands of time
There is so much more I would love to have done
But in your dear heart you will know
The love that comes from your son

May God keep you safe forever
In His bosom where there is no pain
Give me a smile each day from the heavens
Until united we will meet once again.

Sid Harris

MY MOTHER

Life started when I came into the world
My mother's smile easily purled
A new blessing with love and hope
Big world stretched ahead full of scope
Mother and baby both doing well
Nurse over the moon the birth went so swell

Laughter and smiles on every face
Gran and Grandpa a new baby to embrace
Mother the toast of friends and neighbours
With no difficulties during her labours
Homeward bound, a special journey now over
Family gathered together everyone in clover

Love and affection my mother poured on me
Nothing too much effort everyone could see
When I was five she ferried me to school
She believed learning such an essential tool
For making headway in life right from the start
A shoulder to cry on Mother also gave her heart.

Family the foundation for the future coming in sight
Mother's love and devotion the mainstay the light
Happiness matured and grew like buds on a rose
Always gave me a kiss before I went for repose
Memories forever will last guiding my way
A boy's best friend his mother at hand every day

Wonderful things I learnt on my mother's knee
Have carried me upward like a bird flying free
Married now with a young family of my own
Opportunity to return all the joy I have known
Grandma her affection and love still in full bloom
Everlasting an example for young people to groom.

Norman S Brittain

FOR YOU MUM

'Mother I love you, Mum, I really care'
Those special words, we seldom share
I want you to know they are truly meant
Like the happy times we have always spent

Your generous nature, your gentle kindly way
Fond memories of you, in my heart will stay
You are always thoughtful in all that you do
My life has been much richer because of you

When I am sad and lonely, you're my best friend
The things you do for me, there is no end
You're there at my side when I am unwell
Share all my secrets, promising never to tell

Mum, you are so special, you're quite unique
How you brighten my day when things become bleak
I want to say thank you for all that you've done
Especially for being such a wonderful mum.

Linda Brown

Memory Lane

A house full of laughter and laundry,
Garden strewn with toys.
A life spent on family,
Husband, two girls, three boys.

Never more than two feet
From the cooker or the sink,
A total genius
At removing ink!

Scrubbing the nappies
With blocks of Sunlight soap,
Hung on a washing line
Made of blue rope.

Skinned knees and elbows,
Split lips and stubbed toes,
Mumps, chickenpox, measles,
An odd bead up the nose.

We suffered all these ailments
At one time or another.
Trying to feed me porridge
While washing down my brother.

Chasing you with seaweed
Up the pebbly beach.
Showing you a tadpole,
Pretending it was a leech.

Woodbine in one hand,
Face cloth in the other.
Bubbling pot upon the stove,
A snapshot of my mother.

Norah Nelson

EMMA'S MUM

Fifteen years ago, I was a mum,
I thought my life had just begun,
With her beautiful face and bright blue eyes,
At last my Emma had just arrived.

A few days later, tests did discover,
Emma's heart was ill, she would not recover,
I took her home so she could die,
I was her mum, all I could do was cry.

My children here are now growing up fast,
Their childhood days, just do not last,
A mother's love grows every day,
To be there and care for them, in every way.

To be a mum, you have to know,
That sooner or later, you have to let go,
To teach your children to be good and caring,
For them to understand, that life is for sharing.

Fifteen years ago, I had to be strong,
Even though I thought life was totally wrong,
I was honoured to be a mum, for the very first time,
To know that I am Emma's and she is mine.

Emma is in Heaven, that I am sure,
Such a lovely baby, so good and so pure,
All my children are doing so fine,
Between Heaven and here, there is no line.

>Fifteen years ago, my life had just begun,
>That is when I first became a mum.

Pearl Devereux

FOR MY MOM, WITH LOVE

A soft and gentle sigh
A whisper passed my hair
Did I just imagine it
Or are you really there?

In depths of thought a memory lingers
Of deep love and understanding
When did it go, and why?
It happened in the closure of your eyes.

Something died in all of us
The day that we lost you
You were the centre of our family
The pivot, through and through
We all lost a part of us, as well as losing you.

We tried our best to rally round
And care for one another
Something's missing from our team
And that's our precious mother.

So when you look down and see us
Distant and apart
Send your guiding angels round
To mend each and every heart.

I love you, Mom, and miss you so
Every waking day
I wish with all my heart and soul
That you were here today.

I will always treasure the times we shared
The love you gave and the way you cared
You loved us all and showed the way
We should live our life, day by day.

Jacqui Beddow

FOR MY MOTHER

Throughout my life I have received
So many gifts from those that care,
But it's only now as years grow long,
I appreciate the value there.

For a gift when given selflessly,
Expecting nothing in return,
Becomes a lesson in humility,
That perhaps we all should learn.

To me, the finest gift of all,
A gift that no one ever sees,
I've had with me throughout my life,
My happy childhood memories.

Bob Crossley

MUM - SERVER

My mum was a chip shop server
I used to go to work with her
Initially - to observe her

She used to serve with such speed and ease
Whatever your order - a smile came with 'Please'
Fish and chips, cake buttie, chips and mushy peas

In those days - for it's many a year ago
When the first kisses of an autumn age - for mum, were far away
When I was a small boy - I dreamed of great adventures at night
When my gift at words was just an easy test at school

I used to stand on a box behind the counter
A little wooden platform that once contained spuds
I could see above the top - to welcome customers to the shop

The fish fryer was a man called Barry - I don't think he ever married
A fat jolly man betrothed to his job
He'd batter and fry as he sang a happy tune - closing time came
Far too soon
'More chips Barry and put in a special'

Mum would take your order
I'd get paper and she'd pass it over
Paper, that's right!
None of your plastic tray rubbish
In those days - greaseproof bags and new sheet magic

I used to wrap piping red-hot delicacies
Mum had taught me how to do this
Pass your food
A smile - ruffled hair and change
Oh, how times have changed

If I was good - if I was lucky
If I wrapped without a fuss and you were in a hurry
A tip would be mine
Not much, 10p - sometimes 20p

At the end of the day - mid afternoon
I'd go home with my tips and Mum
Like Barry - I'd sing a happy tune.

G Knapton

LAI YUNG

You left us at fifty-two
there were nine of us
and we have only seven left now

You were the princess of Grandmother
you had only one brother
She treated both of you very well
especially spoilt you a lot

Though Grandmother was not rich
you never suffered from hunger
not even during wartime

Many young men wanted to have you as their lover
yet you chose my father
from romance to nightmare
too many responsibilities
too young to take them up

Here's your motto
Never get married with a wrong guy
and raise bad children

One day I suddenly recognised
though your days were even harsher
after the death of our father
you never committed suicide

I feel very grateful
I remember how safe to sleep with you
and how sweet to cool you down with a fan

Mother, my dear, thank you

Mei Yuk Wong

FOR MY MOTHER
(A villanelle)

My thoughts return to happy childhood days,
And to the gift of love my mother gave;
The memory went with me through
          all my wandering ways.

Her love, whichever with me stays,
Gave me such strength and taught me to behave;
My thoughts return to happy childhood days.

Through trials of life, her wisest words always
Stayed with me, helped me to be brave;
The memory went with me through
          all my wandering ways.

So many years have passed, yet still her gaze
Followed and loved me, my worst faults forgave;
My thoughts return to happy childhood days.

I hold my mother in my heart always,
I see her smile, I see her loving wave;
The memory went with me through
          all my wandering ways.

My mother, worthy of the highest praise,
Will never be forgot, our memories we'll save;
My thoughts return to happy childhood days,
The memory went with me through
          all my wandering ways.

Anne James

POEMS FOR MUM

Why are you always nice to others?
This includes talking to your brothers
So why do you talk to me as if I'm a child
When we both know I don't run wild?

How come you think of my sister more than me
When, it is her you hardly ever see?
You think she is the one that's always there
For I know you think that I don't care
Every time you throw an insult
We feel like using a catapult.

Also you talk to me as if I'm only ten
Well, Mum, I am asking you to think again
And remember how old I really am
Plus I don't believe in being really glam.

This is where I should wallow in my glory
For this would normally be a very nice story
You never agree with anything I say, or do
And I could say the same about you.

But I keep my thoughts to myself
Where perhaps I could kick up a stink
And say what I really think
I wish once in a while
Instead, make me smile

You like to get at me for some reason or other
Then sometimes I think why do I bother?
At times you will say I want this, I want that
Instead of having a motherly chat.

Coleen Bradshaw

HARD LINES

Streaks of white clouds form
gentle arms in the skies
gentle arms that seem
to hold me . . . come near me
sing to me lullabies
narrate long stories
'cause I am
listening, waiting
hoping . . .
to feel what I've never felt
gentle embraces
of a mother's arms.

Nayyer Ali

MY TREASURE

From the very moment I was created, you have been there
With unconditional love and support; showing you care
You are the best thing in my life; you are my treasure
The one person always there through the pain and the pleasure

I love you with all of my heart and my soul
Without you my life would be a black hole
I marvel at the sheer wonder and splendour that is you:
You are a beautiful flower that blooms the whole year through

I am a reflection of you: a sculpture you have carved
And I admire you so much for the person you are
I love your kindness, generosity and sense of fun
Your smile is always as warm and as bright as the sun

I don't need to look for anyone else;
I am content with just you and myself
Because it happened to be so, in a twist of fate
That as God dealt out souls, he made yours my mate

I am grateful for every minute that we spend together
My only wish being that it could last forever
But when the time comes for the two of us to part
You know I'll have to carry on with a very heavy heart

And even when that day comes that I most fear
I'll know that you are still always here
Surrounding me with love in all that I do
From that day on when I must live without you.

Christina Marie Dunworth

TO MY LIFE'S GIVER

Your eyes have an inner light
That brightens your lovely features
And any time I look at you
I can foresee the future
Time that relentlessly
Makes youth disappear
Has been lenient with you,
Indeed it has, my dear.
Yours has remained unfaded
And will shine through the years
Like a beacon of beauty
Till the end of your days . . . !

V Malavolta

MOTHER

I will never forget you
Even in this place
None speak about you
I will stay present
In this space
Which your heart reserves for me
I will be there
Not ideal, but someone
Who never put a full stop
To a story of love.
Which is kept far
From speeches of those
Fall in the traps of slander
Who never knew pain which give me
Your absence in silence.

Mack Senge

MOTHER'S POEM

From my day of birth till the day I die,
My mum will be the star of my sky,
The light of my life, she's in my heart,
I know we will never ever part,
Through my times of trouble and stress,
My mum's the person who stops the mess,
Like a rose in the summer, she's the beauty of the land,
She will always be there to hold my hand,
Like the grass shining with morning dew,
My mum will always help me through,
Like a diamond glimmering in the bright, bright sun,
You'll always be my number one,
After I had my near-death crash,
I felt like nothing, I felt like trash,
When I woke in the hospital bed that night,
I saw an angel sparkling bright,
The angel was you, standing over me,
The smile on your face was all I could see,
The light you shine is what woke me,
Mind out of body, I was free!
I love you with all my soul and heart,
I know we will never ever part,
The light in my life, the star in my dreams,
You're always there to stop my screams,
All through my life, my angel is you,
You're my determination that will get me through,
Forever and ever I'll always love you,
You keep my heart and soul so true.

Gary Morton

BARBARA

Kind and pleasant to be around,
Always willing to give a hand.
So generous, she'd give her last pound,
Her home-made lasagne, the best in the land.

Works hard as a cardiac technician,
Touching many lives from 9 to 5.
Yet never looks for recognition,
In her role of keeping them alive.

Her strong worth ethic admired by all,
Hardly a day's rest in thirty years.
She'd come to your aid if she had to crawl,
Just when you need help, Barbara appears.

Bakes cakes for everyone's birthday,
Whether they are one or one hundred.
To your heart she knows the way,
'Friendly to all,' I've heard it said.

Proud of her husband's Jewish roots,
Never takes the Lord's name in vain.
As a mum-in-law, she's a Beaut,
A better friend than Barbara you couldn't gain.

Private chauffeur to her grandson Paul,
Meets him with a smile at school.
At the end of the phone whenever he calls,
Her worth? Priceless - as a precious jewel.

Laura Maxwell

A Mother's Day Ode To A Special Mum

D earest Mother, my special friend
O ne special 'thank you' I do send
R emembering how you loved, cared and looked after me
I shall always treasure those loving memories
S o precious and beautiful like you

G ive anything to see your warm smiling face
R each out and give you a kiss
A happy Mother's Day, my dearest mother
Y ou are very sadly missed.

Sharyn Waters

MUM

My mum raised all six of us,
I am the eldest child.
She taught us rules
That we still use,
Like 'be smart and clean',
'Smile and be polite'.
They still live on
And in our own.
Mums are special.
When I was ill,
She was always there
With a comforting smile,
And cheery words.
She has had a lot of pain
These years as Dad died.
Despite this she always laughs
And keeps us sane.
That's my mum!

Gillian Robson

Mum
(To Lorna Mclean)

To me you're like an angel,
That's fallen from the sky,
You came to live as a mortal,
But you still have magic in your eye.
You have a special touch,
Only you can have,
It can make me cry with joy,
Or make me laugh and laugh.
You make me really happy,
Just by being yourself,
When it comes to picking mums,
I'd take you off the shelf.
I love you very much,
You make my life complete,
Others mums have no chance,
They shouldn't bother to compete.
Because no one can beat you,
You alone stand strong,
You're the best of them all,
Because you alone are my mum.

Ruth Mclean (11)

THANK YOU MUM

Thank you, Mum, for guiding me,
On the road to the person I'm growing up to be.
A girl who is capable and whose spirit is free.
A person who cares for people,
More than I care for me.
A citizen who understands others and their individual needs,
Always considering what is important,
And proving this by my deeds.
Thank you, Mum,
I only want to be,
As good as the woman,
Who has always taken care of me.

Sophie Mir (10)

MY MUM

No poem could ever explain
How wonderful you are to me
You're everything that's beautiful
And everything I want to be

No sonnet could ever express
The place that you have in my heart
I've often attempted to tell you
But somehow I never can start

No story could ever recount
The memories of things that we've done
The years that have passed spent together
You made sure were filled up with fun

No picture could ever convey
The image of you that I see
When I think of your lovely example
And the way that you've made me 'me'

No daughter could ever expect
When she's older she'll ever become
As clever and loving as you are
You wonderful, beautiful mum.

Ester Golding-Webb

MOTHER'S TOUCH
(In honour of my mother, Lou)

Once upon a daffodil
When mothers hit the Earth
They learned how to wash the dishes
And how to light the hearth

They learned what is best
For their little lad
And what their little princess likes
And how to make her glad

Then one of the little mums
Although her hair was wild
She was the best of them
At looking after a child

She knew how to surprise them
On a birthday morning
And how you must put them to bed
As soon as they start yawning

She learned that she should keep a pet
To make her children smile
And that means not for a day or two
You must keep it for a while!

She knew how to tuck them into bed
To make them warm and cosy
And wake them in the morning
Although they may be dozy!

And now you must know
Her name is Louise
She taught her children Elle and Ed
Not to slap or tease

And this training, you know
Is called the *'mother's touch'*.
And that is why I love my mum
Ever so, ever so, ever so much!

Ellen Simmons

POEM FOR MY MUM
(From her proud daughter)

'My mum is the kind of woman
that I hope to become.'

Janice Cameron

MUM

My mum is the best
Out of all the rest
She's sweet and kind
And full of zest

She taught me manners
And how to cook
And how to make
The best of my looks

She encouraged me
Through all the stages
Of life's long journey
Through the ages

With lots of cuddles
And kisses too
After all these years
We've shared a few

With a heart full of love
And a smile like the sun
This magnificent woman
Is my mum.

Pamela Holt

AN ANGEL WITH GOD'S GIFT

From the midnight sky, a million stars shine every night,
from the azure blue, a radiant sun shines ever bright.
From earth, black as coal, grows nature's colours,
                        more beautiful than can compare,
I see all these things and know it is you, it is you that I see there.

It is now that I am older that I see things I have missed,
remembering the cuddles and the hurt that you have kissed.

Never have you stopped doing all those things you do,
you dissolve all my troubles and turn my grey skies blue.

You are an angel with God's gift, sent with colours from above,
you are full of strength and beauty, patience, warmth and love.
It is you that I aspire to and push myself to be,
as wonderful to my children as you always are to me!

All my love
   Nicola.

Nicola Fulstow

MOTHER

You brought me from my cradle
With your loving arms of care
I felt your warmth surround me
Your love was everywhere
So safely you watched o'er me
In that hug I felt no fear
Always there to comfort
My darling mother dear

With love and understanding
We got through the many years
Lots of hugs and kisses
Sometimes laughter, sometimes tears
I think of all the love you gave me
And now that you're not here
Today I miss you more than ever
My darling mother dear.

Shirley May Croxford

MY MUM

Mum, she was all I had,
Never knew a dad.
He went to war in '41,
'Lost in action' they said.
To this day don't know what went on,
Just me, Mum and bro,
From Lincs to Liverpool we did go.
We struggled, why, I wondered, didn't she do better?
Fix up the house, write that letter,
Later, a bionic gran,
No knitting or rocking chair in her plan.
Amusements, fags, a drink at the local,
I became very vocal,
Wanted to change her, rearrange her day,
One windy March, she went away,
'Mum,' I cried, then I knew,
All the brass in the world can't bring her back to you,
Mum in Heaven, far from home,
On your special day, I weep alone.

Elizabeth Marshall

MOTHERING SUNDAY

Mothering Sunday is the time of year,
When I think of my mother,
As I was one of her seven children.
I remember how she worked
Very hard looking after us all.
She baked her own bread.
Every meal was made from
The vegetables from the garden.
She knitted our jumpers, and socks,
And made all our clothes.
There was nothing she couldn't do.
That's how I remember my mother.

A F Hiscocks

The Very Greatest

I bring to you the very latest:
My mum is the very greatest.
That is why I take this time,
To put down this very rhyme.

She's made my life a whole lot better,
And for that I'll never forget her.
Our relationship is abnormally great,
And anyone could debate,
That it's like holy matrimony,
But not so long and not so phoney!

When I'm ill or in time of need,
My mum's there to help and feed;
I lie down in my bed,
My mum sits and wipes my head.

If I'm upset or have some problems,
My mum's there to help me solve them.
Offering a shoulder to cry on and a tissue,
Alongside a hug and a kiss too.

A hard life travels right behind her,
But she copes well as a single minder.

She hasn't got much money,
But not to worry!
She tries and tries to fork it out,
To keep us happy, though I doubt,
She realises that you need a lot more,
To be the greatest mother and all.

And for these reasons and much more,
I request a great encore!
I think we should celebrate,
The fact that my mum is so great.

I've given to you the very latest,
Told you that my mum's the very greatest,
That is why I took this time,
To put down this very rhyme.

I love you Mum!

Toby Harwin (12)

A Mother's Love Is Worth Cherishing

Cushioning the blow,
When the knocks of life
Laid me low
Humiliating self,
I wouldn't let go,
Holding onto the crab
Now and then my mother comes
To stabilise my view
Struck down again
She builds me up, 'Princess,
The beast wasn't worth it!' she cries,
And with sea-frosted glazed eyes
Overflowing, I rub with knuckles as she watches,
The mascara spread,
Channelling over lashes
Into black lakes and streams,
'Poor panda eyes,' she said,
Handing me the mirror
Where reflected black pools of laughter
Ripple to the surface,
And the thoughts of my painful parting, dry up,
The well-oiled sea subsides with the tide,
While my mother's love remains anchored,
Until the sea path is ready to brave once more.

Catherine Keal

A POEM FOR MUM

My mum is very sweet and always caring.
She worries about me when I am in school.
She makes sure that I get where I am going
On time so that I don't feel like a fool.

She cares whenever I pick on my cat.
She cares whenever it or I get hurt.
She cares whenever I score a goal in football.
She cares about the buttons on my shirt.

But, best of all, my mum loves all of us
Who live with her, both when we're good and bad.
She makes me happy with a hug and kiss
And holds my hand whenever I am sad.

You are my mum and my friend,
Which is unusual.
Somehow our characters must blend:
Your wisdom and my will.

I turn, and you are there for me;
I speak, you understand.
I feel cared for, but also free;
You lead but don't command.

I am fortunate that I was born
To someone just like you;
I love you, not just as my mum,
But for what you are and do.

Matthew Willbye (15)

Mum

Just a few words to thank you Mum
For all the things that you have done
You work so hard all of the year
And we always know that you are here.

These thoughts are from us, all three
Liam, Kaitlin and Lucy
We love you always, don't you ever doubt
Even when sometimes you tend to shout.

Anyway, Mum, what we wanted to say
Is hope you have a lovely Mother's Day
We know you love us all year round
And that's us four ever bound.

Tony Turner

MOTHER

Will you kiss it better Mother,
Like you did in days gone by?
Will you take away the heartache,
For sure nothing missed your eye?

If tears were steps to Heaven,
The ones you've shed for me,
Would pass that place quite easily,
And find eternity.

So if I'm always in a hurry,
And ever thoughtless be,
No brighter star lights up God's Heaven,
Than my own darling Mammy.

Windsor Hopkins

A Mother's Touch

Her hands can gently wipe away a tear,
Bring comfort, guidance, and still a nameless fear,
Sometimes they chastise,
Show impatience or despair,
Then, with love
Enfold a trembling form
To show they care. Her hands are just a part
Of a loving, caring mother.

Lil Bordessa

Being A Mother

We rush to the place where their cry is heard
And are at their beck and call;
We patiently listen to every word
Of the tale they wish to recall.
We lovingly teach them to fasten their shoes
And coats as to school they go,
And impatiently wait to hear their news -
Was it plasticine, clay or dough?
The years march on and we're filled with pride
At the strengths they are beginning to show,
Their weaknesses we do not chide
But encourage their talents to grow.
When boy/girl relationships come on the scene
We quietly wait to advise,
Our shoulder is there on which they can lean
If they're willing to listen, they're wise.
In their pain and their heartaches we get alongside
And should friendships come to an end
Then we wipe away tears, which *we've* inwardly cried,
On us they can always depend.
But the very best gift we can give them
Along with the present of love
Is the gift of prayer offered for them
To our Heavenly Father above.
Committing them daily should be our goal
He is wiser than any other;
With Him to share the precious role
It's a privilege being a mother.

Mary Davies

ONE IN A MILLION - MY MUM

My mum, she was one in a million
Always there for me
My mum, she had a really hard time
Six hungry mouths to feed.
My mum, she never envied, her wants were very few
My mum's words echo in my mind, they were so very true
She scrubbed and cleaned and I often saw her work
                                      throughout the night
Yet very early at the crack of dawn she always seemed so bright
She would wrap her arms around me and tell me not to cry
She would wipe the tears from my eyes till every one was dry
She's resting now in paradise where angels take their rest
Because while she lived upon this Earth she was one of the best.

Lorraine A Robinson

Mum

I can't touch you or feel you or hear you,
I can't smell you or see you or be with you,
Because you just aren't here anymore.
For nearly fifty years you were there for me
In everything I did, good or bad
And now there is no view of you.
You were the best friend I ever had.
I try to recall your voice, your smile,
The way you walked and stood
Now all I have is a photograph
To remember all the good.
I'll try to make you proud of me
And bad things I will shun,
For there has never ever been,
Such a finer *mum!*

Susan Jenner

MOTHER

Just a quick poem
To say to my mother
You're the best in the world
I wouldn't want another

You're not just a mum
You're a very good friend
I hope our relationship
Never comes to an end

You've taken good care of me
Ever since I was born
You're my sunshine, you're my rain
You're my dusk, you're my dawn

Thank you for everything
Is what I'm trying to say
I love you so much
More and more every day.

Gary Bil

MY MAM

Toil and sweat, she went on and on, we were hard work, the eight of us.
Shopping and cooking and cleaning, never stopping,
Only when sat on a bus.
Going for clothes, for food, her shopping bags full,
Her arms aching and weary, and already planning in her mind, tea.
We ran to the bus stop, 'What have you got? Let's look in your bag
    and see.'
Eight hungry mouths to feed, as well as her own.
My dad having been down the pit all day,
Would be tired and hungry, just like us, waiting for food like a child.
No one stopped to think of me mam, she must have felt like going wild.
No time for herself to find the person she must have been,
Except in the bath with her bath cubes we bought her for Christmas.
Then, only then, maybe she felt like a queen.
Even though all these things must have made her feel like
    running away,
She always had time to stop and play.
Her singing I loved when I was a child,
I knew then she was happy as she could be.
She must have known it was all worth it,
When she looked at my sisters, brothers and me.
Now she's gone, but the memories so real,
And now all that I feel
Is love!

Cindy Webster

I Love My Mum

I really do love my mum
For she's very special to me,
She picks me up when I am down
And chases away life's misery.
She was always there when I was little
To give me a kiss and a cuddle,
And even now she'll always see
Me safely through life's muddle.
My mum is my number one fan
She supports me in every way,
And now that I have my own children
She helps me more and more each day.
There's nothing I ever want for,
Nothing that I ever go without,
Because that is what my mum thinks
Her role in my life is about.
My mum has a certain calmness,
She has great pride and dignity,
She is much loved by friends and relations
And many others in our small community.
Yes, my world will certainly be darker
When God has called her up above,
But I know that when my time here is over
She'll come to collect me with love.

Trudy Marie Burge

MOTHER

Mother, thinking back to the memories we knew,
best friends then, were me and you.
I must have been a burden coming so late,
you never complained at any rate.
Spoilt free, but loved the same,
you were always there, you always came
You could hurt now and then,
it taught me about why and when.
Oh Mother, you taught me oh, so much,
your spirit will always be in touch.
Your love was always easy to hold,
a mother's love is just like gold.
The sacrifice I never knew,
all this came from only you.
Now you've gone to God's golden shore,
I've got to know you more and more.
A loner were you, through and through,
I'm proud to have some of it too.
But friendly and thoughtful, you were the best,
I could go on, but you know the rest.
Right now I'm smiling with a gentle nod
for I know, you've another life at the foot of God.

Hugh H Foulkes

MOTHERING SUNDAY

M other of mine
O nly one of a kind
T he love she gives
H er unselfish heart lives
E very day she is there
R eassuring with care
I n all she provides
N o one she divides
G iving, taking no sides.

S uch devotion and love
U nending is her light from above
N othing seems to give pain
D ay after day she seems the same
A rms open with love that's endless
Y et always there, always to bless.

Alan J Morgan

MUM

In a soft bubble of life fluid, you carried me and cushioned me
With love.
A warm ache blooms, cries and echoes float through the blue.
As I surface from deep water, a pale light breathes on me and
I join you in life's garden.
By your gentle hands, I grow under a ceiling of clouds.
You propose the questions, give the light that creates,
From pictures and words and useless objects that mean the Earth.
When the light starts to fade, you are there, giving me time,
Listening and caring.
Your smile fills me with joy,
Your tremor is my earthquake.
I look forward to seeing you at the end of every day, and I love you!

Jack Thurgar

VISITING MY MUM

She watches TV till nine, then goes to bed
Before she falls asleep in the chair.
Sometimes sleep gets to her first, but I leave unsaid
The words unneeded when you care.
A gentle shake, a smile, are all she needs,
Just to know I am there for a while.
Tomorrow I return to where, sadly, my road leads,
A place far away from my mother's smile.

Next month I'll return, she knows I will,
Another visit to what is still home,
From where, slowly, my life I distil,
Like rainwater, through the dark loam
Of this place far away from the house of my birth;
This place to which I do not belong:
Return to her smile and the welcoming earth
Of her garden: her home, where I do belong.

Kevin Godfrey

MOTHER'S DAY

We present our cards, with flowers and gifts
To show you that we care
For you are someone special
No other can compare

You are the heartbeat of the home
The jewel in the crown
The one we can rely on
To never let us down

You never fail to do your best
Your heart is true and tender
Selflessly you give your love
And we in turn remember

For all the things that you have done
To help us through 'Life's way'
'This is our chance to thank you Mum
On your own special day.'

Carol Kaye

SHE IS NICE TO ME

I never know what you're worth
Until I see a pregnant woman
I never know what you are worth
Until I see a pregnant woman in labour
I never know what you are worth
Until I see a motherless child
I never know what you are worth
Until I am hungry and you are not there.

Mama I say thank you
For carrying me in your womb for nine months.
I say I am grateful
For the training you gave me
And you are still giving me.
I appreciate the love you have for me
Your love for me is likened to God's love
Without you I would have been nothing.

Ogbodo John Obinna

A BELATED MESSAGE
(Mary Isabella Pass 11th May 1908 - 24th February 1982)

Mum, you were my rock,
Dependable, always at hand,
To protect and shield me,
A shelter from life's storms,
Your last words,
'Take care of yourself,'
And then you slipped away,
And I was alone,
My world came tumbling down,
And left a void that only a mother can fill.

Memories were all that I had,
At the time I was afraid that these would fade,
I never gave you many hugs and kisses,
And seldom said how much I loved you,
But I think you knew, as mothers do,
A long time has passed since,
And the memories are still with me,
For they were the precious threads,
That interlink between a mother and child,
And these cannot be broken.

I loved you in the life we shared,
And I love you now,
Though you are out of sight,
I know you still watch over me,
And feel your presence around,
I miss seeing you even after all these years,
On this Mother's Day, I would like to say,
'Thank you for everything,
But, most of all, for being,
My special mum.'

Ann G Wallace

MUM

Although long gone, I'll ne'er forget,
That kindly face, no penny of debt;
Her life so hard, so loyal, so true,
How much for her a rest was due.

From early days the care was great,
The love we had, it was top rate;
Our clothes so clean, all pressed and neat,
Mum was so proud of all our feats.

The day when raid, and bombs came down,
Mum got on bike and came to town;
She clambered over rubble and stones,
No thought was given to her own bones.

When service came to our King in place,
Mum kept in touch with letters and grace;
When home on leave, the welcome great,
Mum made us proud, she was first-rate.

Through college years, support so great,
Our Cumbrian wedding was great date;
When children came, Mum's love supreme,
The grandchildren, for her, a dream.

Dad's life on farm meant work so hard,
Mum strove to help, she kept her guard;
With final day of work on farm,
Dad dropped down dead, it raised alarm.

For Mum alone, life was so bleak,
We made our journeys, week by week;
Mum's care, concern and love stayed great,
She's now in Heaven, with key to gate.

John Paulley

LOVE

I am a mum,
Though I wasn't that good,
I didn't do things,
Perhaps as I should,
But now I am wiser,
I'm trying again,
To be a bit better,
Well that is my aim.
We've all made mistakes,
We learn from the past,
Should stop and think,
And not go so fast.
But my love was unending,
Patient and true,
For the child that I had,
I did all I could do.

M Wlicox

Requiem For Mum

Why are they laughing and talking?
Don't they care that my mother has died?
That we have just left the hospital
Where my sister and I have just cried?

Why can't they see our sorrow?
We've just lost the one we held dear
We're holding our grief to our bosoms
While they talk of bingo and beer.

For weeks she has lain in the hospital
Wracked with such cancerous pain
But at last she is out of her suffering
Though our hearts are just breaking in twain.

I suppose life goes on ad infinitum
Everything passes, we're told
But Mother had always been with us
It's really no fun getting old.

But I'm sure there's a new angel in Heaven
Leading the choir in song
And watching forever over us
As she did, our whole life long.

Jean Wallington

MY MUM

From the moment I was born
Mum, you cherished me with love
I was your special angel
Sent from Heaven above

You cared for me
In so many ways
I'll remember always
Through my days

You sacrificed
Your all for me
From school
To university

So now I've grown
I'd like to say
A thank you
In my special way

I studied hard
I got the grade
Your little star
You brightly made.

K Christie

A LOVE THAT MUST BE TRUSTED

A mother is a loving word, so pleasing to the ear,
Her kindness is a little song, which brings a world of cheer.
A mother is a friendly face, when one is growing old,
And radiates a glowing warmth, when all the world is cold.
A mother is a helping hand, across a busy street,
So thoughtful in the way she smiles, which makes all joy complete.
Her kindness is that something, that no one really sees,
But how immense the difference, when she always aims to please.
When I was very, very small, a little girl of four,
She used the pick the daisies in the field outside our door.
She chose to pick the biggest ones to weave her lovely chain,
The dewdrops shone like diamonds, in the early morning rain.
She used to thread the daisies just kneeling in the grass
Whilst overhead in beauty, the clouds of summer passed.
The flowered chain of daisies she threaded through her hair,
Those days were filled with wonder, without a single care.

It only seemed like yesterday, that I went off to school,
My mother sat and worried so, but still appeared cool.
Remembering all the sports days, the pride when I had won,
Shedding tears of happiness, of laughter and of fun.
The moment that I started work, she gave me sound advice,
To try to be successful, my hands they held the dice.
Another chapter in my life was just about to start,
Success my mother wished me which came right from her heart.
With springtime in our hearts and a twinkle in our eye
We'll always love each other, which no one can deny.
There's magic in our world and special dreams to hold,
And though the years relentless, we'll let them just unfold.
Dreams of happy childhood surround me every day,
Thank you dearest Mother, for showing me the way.

Marjorie Picton

MOTHER'S BLESSING

A mother's wish seen in her eye,
her face crumples, as she starts to cry.
She looks upon her daughter who was once so small,
now she feels her love is not returned at all.

The gentle breaking of their intertwined days,
as her daughter leaves to go her own ways.
Inside a part of her motherhood is going,
as the relationship changes to enable growing.

A natural realisation of a natural part,
of separation as she sees her daughter depart.
Her daughter looks back with sad wet eyes,
they both blow a kiss as they say their goodbyes.

A sadness in the air as life moves on,
both fearful of what life will be without the other one.
But as her daughter leaves to make way on her own,
they both smile in the realisation that home will always be home.

Rebecca Guest

A MINER'S WIFE, MY MOTHER

A miner's wife, my mother, Julie.
Steadfast, stocky: solid as a rock.
Though poor, she walked proud and tall,
Her clothes bought from a second-hand stall.
She married Dad back in January 1941,
She already some months pregnant,
With me, John, her firstborn son.
She, then thirty-four, her Bill, forty-one.
Not kids, this couple, my dame and sire.
Nor beautiful people these,
Yet they fulfilled each other's needs.
An older love it's said, the best of all.
Their love born out of shared hardship.
My dad from childhood, prone to asthma.
The mine's coal dust made him sick.
He was an underground railroad layer.
Which the trucks ran on down the pit.
Mother, before her quickie marriage,
Had been a skilled pottery gilder.
In fact with her craft apprenticeship,
When employed on a piecework rate,
Could earn more than my old dad.
Later she bore him a second son.
The 1950s, less hardship, she back to work.
Electricity installed in our terraced house,
Followed by oilcloth, and new carpets,
Cheap furniture bought for the parlour,
My brother, Michael, sent to grammar school.
She has been gone now these seven years.
Yet still I miss my mum; Dad's old girl.

John Pegg

THE QUEEN OF CREATION BE SHE

To know not the concept of mother
Is too long for the substance I miss
For who could take the place
Of the one woman ever
That would lovingly spare me
A motherly kiss?

In times of unease
Ill-health and despair
Ever eager to please
Giving strength and repair
Advice and good guidance
You'd selflessly share
And would always but always
But always
Be there

I'd have someone to talk to
And drive round the bend
Whom to every single day
A poem would I send
To show her what she made
And how I turned out
In the end
But mainly in my dream of dreams
My one forgiving friend

The Queen of creation
So perfect she be
The whole of my being
Be gifted by she
Yet I learn to live with what I've got
And only dare to dream of that I've not.

Mark Anthony Noble

MOTHERS

They do not ask for hair so grey
That's sprinkled fine with gold
Or love that's seen from sightless eyes
Their children's pain untold

Or furrowed brow like farmer's field
The worries of the world
Or hands so red from wringing hard
At troubles . . . 'unprepared'

They do not ask for big red eyes
From crying through the night
An aching heart or crown of thorns
When life turns out its light

They do not ask for weary feet
Nor head in hands to hold
Or misty eyes through which to see
The misery unfold

They do not ask to toss and turn
On bed of broken glass
A pillow made of sharp barbed wire
Or their own youth to pass

They do not ask in valleys dark
To simply walk alone
No letter saying, 'How are you?'
No ringing telephone

No, mothers are a special breed
Of person, don't you know?
They never need instruction books
Their feelings then to show

It's like they're simply always there
A parachute, I'd say
No matter what our troubles are
Just pull the cord . . . 'today'

But when we're young and we can't wait
To break the family chain
To go away and see the world
We simply forget pain

It's nice to know that come what may
Their love grows stronger yet
They did not ask for hair of grey
Don't ever you . . . 'forget'.

R Weedall

MOTHER

Even though she's no longer here, she still remains in my heart
Inside my body, she fills this void, she will never ever depart
Frail and weak in her final years, I loved her very dearly
She always taught me to look at life, constructively and clearly.

Always there when needed, forever providing a meal
Her bread pudding was something else, it made such great appeal
There were never complications, our lives were rich with love
And though we don't see her features, she shines from high above.

She provided a treasure trove of tales, about her younger days
A proud and beautiful woman she was, in just so many ways
Her role as mother and as wife, from this she would never detract
And if we needed a sharp word or two, she would never rescind
                                                         or retract.

Bringing up all her children, made her richer, when life was
                                                      hard and raw
And then of course I came along, and added just one more
I remember her down the terrace, hanging out washing on the line
And from those bright eyes of hers, the sun would seem to shine.

Our Billy and our Ron, they were her special boys
And all the daughters she gave birth to, provided lots of joys
Later lineage provided more fun, as she took small babes in her arms
And one thing she exuded, was the emanating of her many charms.

Later on in life of course, she became weak and very frail
When ascending or dismounting the stairs, holding tightly to the rail
Always sitting by the phone, when she expected the phone to ring
Plenty to hear, an abundance of chat, even then she was suffering.

We all think back to the Golden Wedding, when Brenda came to call
We have our own individual recollections, remembering them
                                                   walking in that hall

The joy on their faces beamed out loud, surprise at this unknown treat
I remember everyone rushing forward, this tiny lady they wanted
                                                                                  to greet.

Finally things took their toll, and she was confined to her bed
I recall one of the final sentences that she ever said,
From taking me in and adding to her own, I was never able to convey
'You took in an addition to your own, and I loved you every day!'

B W Ballard

GRAND GESTURES

I tried to show how much I love you,
But my arms wouldn't stretch enough,
But they might stretch the whole world over,
And still not measure up.

I tried to show how much I love you,
But there isn't enough money to buy,
Something as big, and as bold, and as beautiful,
That it could capture all I feel inside.

I tried to show how much I love you,
But there is no deed so grand,
That I could do it every day,
And make you understand.

I tried to show how much I love you,
With gestures big, fantastic deeds, and money in massive amount,
All the while I did not see,
It's the little things that count.

I try to show how much I love you,
And my arms can stretch to reach right
Around when you need a hug,
All I do is squeeze real tight.

I try to show how much I love you,
And there's just enough money to buy,
A special treat, just now and then,
To get your spirits up again.

I try to show how much I love you,
And there are deeds enough,
Bits and pieces round the house,
That will make your job less tough.

I need no grand gestures to show you that I care,
You know that when you need me, I'll be right there.

Tiffany Little

MY MOTHER

My mother brought me to this world, she cares for me each day,
My mother I love very much, in each and every way.
My mother, I must thank you, for what you've done for me,
You taught me such good morals, to live life and be free.

She'd help me take my first few steps, and raise me if I fell,
She'd comfort me if I did cry, no need for me to tell.
She'd always help when I was stuck with homework, yes it's true,
And always will support me in what I decide to do,

Someone who does the cooking, and the housework every day,
Someone who keeps my clothing clean, I do not need to say,
Someone who tucks me into bed, she worries how I am,
No prizes just for guessing that this someone is my mam.

I'm proud to call her Mum, so thankful and so glad,
I'm always in her thoughts I know, without her I'd be sad,
I'm getting older every day and soon I'll reach the age,
When I'll leave home and say farewell, and turn another page.

As I move on to adulthood, and have to learn myself,
Life's not a bed of roses, cannot buy it off a shelf,
Now friends will come and they will go, that's easy to explain,
Our mothers are our greatest friend, they always will remain.

Robert Basham

MY MOTHER

My beloved mother, how soundly you sleep,
Your face is framed with hair silvery,
Let me kiss your forehead wrinkled,
The lines on your face speak a lifetime's love,
That has lifted me from many failures,
When I was just a small young boy,
You were my friend, philosopher and teacher,
You helped me in all my schoolwork,
And baked my favourite cake always,
You carried the nine-year-old to the doctor,
When the fractured leg made me scream,
When failure in school, disgraced me,
You held me with love close to your bosom,
You kissed me farewell, wiping your tears,
Hugged me close and whispered softly,
'Soon we shall be together my love,
Now you must go to make your career,
My love for you shall cast a ring,
Protecting you from all sorrows,
Let all my merits go with you,
And all your failures and flaws are mine.'
My ambition high, needed wealth,
You sold your jewels and the modest house,
To make me a man with name and fame,
Your sacrifice was unknown before,
Thank you my mother for all you have done,
You are most sacred of all creation,
The Creator made you when he was kind,
And you are love personified.

P K Janaky

A GLIMPSE OF HEAVEN
(A true story)

Mum's heaven was always a garden,
But one day when she was so ill
A priest came to give her a pardon,
To back up the doctor's failed pill.

She lay for three days in a coma,
Though everyone thought she had gone;
Her love and sweet-scented aroma . . .
Returned like a beautiful song.

Mum spoke of her mental adventure,
There was a young man, she revealed.
Her words held no sign of dementia
His voice to her gently appealed.

They'd wandered in gardens with flowers
Caressed by the warmth of May sun;
And pleasured for heavenly hours
Before he had pointed to one . . .

An avenue shaded by fir trees
In evergreen, silver and blue,
Majestically gracing an entrance
To which a bright light glistened through.

He bade her to enter beside him;
The garden of gardens to roam.
But Mother, then gently denied him,
She stated her wish to go home.

Now, science may give us some logic
With subconscious action in mind
Myself, I prefer just to dodge it,
To see what the future may find.

Pearl M Burdock

A Family Treasure

How can I measure a family treasure,
Without getting over-sentimental,
And making the woman I call Mother,
Into some kind of minor deity?
For one must have seen the human heart,
Which once beat beneath her mortal flesh,
Yet I concede that such a person was Julie.
She had endured hardship all her life.
At thirteen, her mother, by the flu, died.
Being the oldest girl forced to leave school,
To care for a brood of young siblings.
Until her father took another wife,
Another set of halflings then ensued.
Endured, to marry my dad at thirty-five.
He, eight years her senior,
Me, her firstborn on the way.
William, my dad, seemed eternally sick.
A chronic asthmatic, and miner to boot.
Scant wages earned in the local pit.
Our house a Victorian end terrace.
Forever damp, full of drying washing,
And scant, hand-me-down furniture.
A son arrived when Dad turned fifty.
Soon after our Queen's coronation,
She returned to work as a pottery gilder.
Redemption followed financial improvements,
Young brother sent to the grammar school.
Years flowed, still she wore second-hand clothes.
Dad having passed away, she, too, grew old.
Now April; on her grave grow blooms of gold.

Julia Pegg

Mum

Mum, you were there the second I was born.
You nurtured, you cared for me, until I grew strong.
The first day of school, I held your hand tight.
Didn't want to let go, or let you out of my sight.

As the school years went on, you struggled so hard.
Teaching me right and wrong, still keeping up your guard.
Times were hard then, it could not have been easy.
Scrimping and scraping, looking after me was your reason.

The teenage years came on, I knew better than you.
Well, that's what I thought; now I know that's not true.
I wasn't the easiest teenager, I gave you such a hard time.
I rebelled more than once, I thought I was fine.

You knew better, I worried you so much.
You were always there, never left me in the lurch.
I let you down Mum, you never gave up.
You were always there for me, always kept in touch.

I'm sorting my life out Mum; it's all thanks to you.
Without your loving or nurturing this dream would not have been true.
I'm writing this poem, to write what I don't say.
I love you, I love you, you'll be proud some day.

Charlene Tate

IOU MUM

My security and safety
My bodyguard and keeper
She has always been there
Right from a cheeky peeper
I have caused her loads of worry
'I am sorry,' just ain't enough
She has pulled me off Death Row
I've never met anyone as tough
She is often in my thoughts
As she has been in my trouble
I guiltily witnessed her disappointment
As I burst bubble after bubble
There just aren't enough words
To describe her everlasting love
In danger and the cold
She protects me like a glove
Only shouts for a reason
Usually as my chaos increases
But when I've left her presence
Her love has picked up my pieces
Most of my problems
Would have seen others crumble
She lovingly repairs the damage
Replacing it with a warning grumble
I've more than tested her patience
Well past the finishing line
I damaged her loving faith
And wrongly cut it fine
My aim is to release her
Of the worry she has for me
Make her proud of her son
For everyone to see
I carry the shame a lot less
With her love when mine was numb

She has never let me down
Just reminded me with more love from Mum
She understands me like no other
And she is the most wonderful mother.

R Bennett

My Fantastic Mum

Closed eyes awaken,
Softness of smoothness,
Featherweight of lightweight,
Frailty of affection,
Instant connection,
Invisible cord of simultaneous love,
Cradled with bonded protection,
Touch so tender,
Pure and sincere,
Heart of two is joined together as one.
Fast beat, erratic and unsteady,
Pulse rate is stabilised to normal,
Tiny arms, tiny legs and tiny feet,
Alive and kicking,
Human kindness embrace.
Blood-stained, red-yellow face,
Newborn flesh to polish clean,
Little finger clasp so tight,
Infant child of Mother to cherish,
Mama's pride and joy!
From a loving son to his fantastic mum.
Thanks for being there,
All of the time,
Wish you were still here,
Miss you lots.
Love you more and more each day,
That goes so quickly past.

Love,
Nigel

Nigel Astell

INFORMATION

We hope you have enjoyed reading this book - and that you will continue to enjoy it in the coming years.

If you like reading and writing poetry drop us a line, or give us a call, and we'll send you a free information pack.

Alternatively if you would like to order further copies of this book or any of our other titles, then please give us a call or log onto our website at www.forwardpress.co.uk

Anchor Books Information
Remus House
Coltsfoot Drive
Peterborough
PE2 9JX
(01733) 898102